Published in the UK by
POWERFRESH Limited
21 Rothersthorpe Crescent
Northampton
NN4 8JD

Telephone   0845 130 4565
Facsimile   0845 130 4563
E Mail   info@powerfresh.co.uk

ISBN 1902929241

Printed in Malta by Gutenberg Press Limited
Powerfresh   February 2002 reprint November 2002

Forty is the age when you stop patting yourself on the head and start under the chin.

Oh to be only half as wonderful as my child thought I was when he was small, and only half as stupid as my teenager now thinks I am.
(*Rebecca Richards*)

When women pass thirty they forget their age. When forty, forget they ever remembered it. (*Ninon de Lenclos*)

You know you've reached middle age when your weightlifting consists merely of standing up. (*Bob Hope*)

39
is a nice age for women,
especially if she happens to be
47.

She claims she just turned 30:
it must have been a U-turn.

Allow me to put the record straight. I'm 46 and have been for some years past.
(*Erica Jong*)

I'm 48 when I wake up in the morning I find my face hanging on the end of the bed.
(*Jill Gascoigne*)

You know you're getting old when everything hurts. And what doesn't hurt doesn't work. (*Hy Gardner*)

I've been 40 and I've been 50 and I can tell you 40 is better.
(*Cher*)

The older I get,
the better I used to be.
(*John McEnroe*)

I'm now at the age where I've got to prove that I'm just as good as I never was.
(*Rex Harrison*)

At the age of 20 we don't care
what the world thinks of us.
At 30 we worry deeply about
what it thinks of us.
At 40 we realise it isn't thinking of
us at all.
(*Herbert Prochnow*)

Children despise their parents until the age of 40, when they suddenly become just like them, thus preserving the pattern.
(*Quentin Crewe*)

There's only one cure for grey hair. The French invented it. It's called the guillotine.

Ageing seems to be the only known way to live a long time, unfortunately.
(*Daniel Auber*)

An archaeologist is the best husband any woman can have. The older she gets, the more interested he is in her.
(*Agatha Christie*)

After 40 a woman has to choose between losing her face or her figure. My advice is to keep your face and stay sitting down.
(*Barbara Cartland*)

She finally admitted she was 40 - but she didn't say when.

I refuse to believe that I'm 52,
even if that makes my children
illegitimate.
(*Nancy Astor*)

It's just as well to be told you're too old at 40; then you're over it. (*Grace Murney Hooper*)

No, it's not great being over 50.
In fact it's like going to the
guillotine.
(*Angie Dickinson*)

She's 46 going on indefinitely.

Now that she's reached 40 she's behaving like a technician at a space station: she's started the countdown.

She'll never live to be 50 - not at the rate she's overstaying 40.

There's a woman who keeps her age very well. So well that she's been 40 for the past 11 years.

One of the hardest decisions in life is wondering when to start middle age.
(*Clive James*)

Thirty is a nice age for a woman -
especially if she happens to be
forty.
(*Phyllis Diller*)

At 40 a woman is just about old enough to start looking younger. (*Katharine Whitehorn*)

When I was 40 my doctor advised me that a man in his forties shouldn't play tennis. I heeded his advice carefully and could hardly wait until I reached 50 to start again.
(*Hugo Black*)

I'm at the age where my back
goes out more than I do.
(*Phyllis Diller*)

Age is a question of mind over matter. If you don't mind, it doesn't matter.
(*Dan Ingman*)

She says she's just reached 40.
I'm wondering what delayed her.

A woman past 40 should make
up her mind to be young,
not her face.
(*Billie Burke*)

She couldn't wait to be forty so that she could get a facelift to make herself look younger.

People ought to retire at 40 when they feel over-used and go back to work at 65 when they feel useless.
(*Carol Anne O'Marie*)

You know you're getting older when you try to straighten out the wrinkles in your socks -and discover you're not wearing any.
(*Leonard Knott*)

Middle age is when you're sitting at home on a Saturday night and the phone rings and you hope it's not for you.
(*Ogden Nash*)

The lovely thing about being 40
is that you can appreciate
25 year old men more.
(*Colleen McCullough*)

Middle age is that time in a man's life when his daydreams centre round a bank manager saying yes instead of a girl.
(*Jane Fonda*)

Most women aren't as young
as they're painted.
(*Max Beerbohm*)

You know you've reached forty when your little red book doesn't have the numbers of old flames anymore, but GPs.

My wife has just turned 34
It's her 43rd birthday.

On my fortieth birthday my son gave, a card saying 'Life begins at 40.
Underneath that message was written in smaller letters 'But so does rheumatism, arthritis, lumbago, sciatica, constipation and myopia'.

To be 70 years young is far more cheerful than to be 40 years old. (*O.W. Holmes*)

I'm not like Jane Fonda or any
of those other women who say
how fabulous they think it is to
turn forty.
The truth is, it's a crock of shit.
(*Cher*)

When a man of 40 falls in love
with a girl of 20 it's not her youth
he's seeking, but his own.
(*Lenore Coffee*)

I believe in loyalty. When a woman reaches an age she likes, she should stick to it.
(*Eva Gabor*)

At 16 I was stupid, insecure and indecisive.

At 25 I was wise, self-confident, prepossessing and assertive.

At 45 I am stupid, confused, insecure and indecisive.

Who would have supposed that maturity is only a short break in adolescence?

(*Jules Pfeiffer*)

This actress I knew, when I was
31, she was 36.
When I got to 40, she was 37.
That must have been some year!
(*Tony Curtis*)

The seven ages of women are:
baby, infant, miss, young woman,
young woman, young woman
and young woman.

At 50 everyone has the face he
deserves.
(*George Orwell*)

When Marlene Dietrich complained to her photographer that he wasn't making her look as beautiful as he used to, he told her, 'I'm sorry, Marlene. but I'm seven years older now'.

An actress once said to Rosalind Russell, 'I dread the thought of 45'. Russell looked at her and said, 'Why - what happened?'

She's been pressing forty so long,
it's pleated.

The secret of staying young is to live honestly, eat slowly and lie about your age.
(*Lucille Ball*)

A doctor told me jogging would add ten years to my life.
I told him, 'Yeah -since I began I feel ten years older'.
(*Lee Trevino*)

At 40 a woman is just about old enough to start looking younger.
(*Katherine Whitehorn*)

"A very old 12".
(*Noel Coward after being asked how a female acquaintance looked after a facelift*)

You know you're getting old when your idea of a hot, flaming desire is a barbecued steak.
(*Victoria Fabiano*)

The really frightening thing about middle age is the knowledge that you'll grow out of it.
(*Doris Day*)

Women over 40 are at their best, but men over 30 are too old to recognise it.
(*Jean Paul Belmondo*)

At my age, the only reason I'd take up jogging again would be to hear heavy breathing. (*Erma Bombeck*)

I am just turning 40, and taking
my time about it.
(*Harold Lloyd at 77 after being
asked his age by a journalist from
The Times*)

Setting a good example for the
children takes all the fun out of
middle age.
(*William Feather*)

Preparing for the worst is an activity I have taken up since I turned 35 and the worst actually began to happen just then.
(*Delia Ephron*)

You know you've reached middle age when you toss up between two alternatives and plump for the one that gets you home by nine oclock.
(*Ronald Reagan*)

Pushing forty?
On the contrary, she's clinging
onto it for dear life!
(*Ivy Compton-Burnett of an
acquaintance*)

Middle age is when work is a lot less fun, and fun is a lot more work.
(*Milton Berle*)

40 is the first time you realise you can't do it the second time.
50 is the second time you realise you can't do it the first time.
(*Mort Sahl*)

Middle age is when everything
new you feel is likely to be a
symptom.
(*Laurence J. Peter*)

The great comfort of turning 40 is
the realisation that you are now
too old to die young.
(*Paul Dickson*)

Middle age is when your age starts to show around the middle.

Middle age is when you bend down to tie your shoelace, and then wonder if there's anything else you can do while you're down there.

Actresses over 40 can generally kiss goodbye to their film careers in Hollywood, but an actor can go on to nearly double that. (*Meryl Streep*)

Every man over 40 is a scoundrel
(*George Bernard Shaw*)

I'm pleased to be here.
Let's face it, at my age I'm
pleased to be anywhere.
(*Ronald Reagan*)

I've been around so long I knew
Doris Day before she was a
virgin.
(*Groucho Marx*)

When I started in show business,
the Dead Sea was only sick.
(*George Burns*)

My age is 39 plus tax.
(*Liberace*)

I was born in 1962.
The room next to me was 1963.
(*Joan Rivers*)

Old age is always 15 years older
than what I am
(*Bernard Baruch*)

As long as you can still be
disappointed, you're still young.
(*Sarah Churchill*)

Zsa Zsa Gabor has just
celebrated the 41st anniversary
of her 39th birthday.
(*Joan Rivers*)

Birthdays only come once a year -unless you're Joan Collins, In which case they only come once every FOUR years.

The best years of Joan Collins life were the ten years between 39 and 40.

The four stages of man are infancy, childhood, adolescence and obsolescence.
(*Art Linkletter*)

There are three signs of old age:
you forget names, you forget
faces, and...
(*Red Skelton*)

Middle age is when it takes you all night to do once what once you used to do all night.
(*Kenny Everett*)

As a graduate of the Zsa Zsa Gabor School of Creative Mathematics, I honestly do not know how old I am.
(*Erma Bombeck*)

First you forget names, then you forget faces. Then you forget to zip your fly. Then you forget to unzip your fly.
(*American baseball manager Branch Rickey on the perils of ageing*)

When you're green you're growing, when you're ripe you're not.
(*Ray Kroc*)

You can order other Little books directly from Powerfresh Limited. All at £1.99 each including postage (UK only)

Postage and packing outside the UK: Europe: add 20% of retail price
Rest of the world: add 30% of retail price

To order any Powerfresh book please call 0845 130 4565

Powerfresh Limited
21 Rothersthorpe Crescent
Northampton NN4 8JD